GRADED
GUITAR SONGS
9 ROCK CLASSICS CAREFULLY ARRANGED FOR BEGINNING LEVEL GUITARISTS

ISBN 978-1-61780-707-7

HAL•LEONARD®
CORPORATION

7777 W. BLUEMOUND RD. P.O. BOX 13819 MILWAUKEE, WI 53213

In Australia Contact:
Hal Leonard Australia Pty. Ltd.
4 Lentara Court
Cheltenham, Victoria, 3192 Australia
Email: ausadmin@halleonard.com.au

Visit Hal Leonard Online at
www.halleonard.com

INTRODUCTION

This book contains arrangements of nine classic rock songs – each specially arranged to make them technically accessible for early stage guitar players, while preserving the authenticity of the original song. A recording of each song is provided to make learning easier. A backing track is also provided for each song, for you to play along to.

The songs were arranged by Tony Skinner and Merv Young, Senior Guitar Examiners from Registry of Guitar Tutors (RGT), and have been designed to reflect the exact requirements of the RGT's Grades 1 to 3 exams in rock guitar playing.

About RGT

RGT, established in the UK in 1992, is the world's largest organization of guitar teachers. In conjunction with its partner London College of Music (established 1887), RGT provides internation-ally-recognized exams in rock guitar, electric guitar, acoustic guitar, bass guitar, classical guitar and popular music theory. Exams start at beginner level and progress to Diploma level for professional players and teachers. RGT exams are held in over 30 countries, including North America.

Benefits of Taking an RGT Exam

- Gain a useful and internationally recognized qualification.
- Find out, via a reliable and independent assessment, what standard your playing is.
- Achieve your playing potential by setting yourself a clear target to aspire to.
- Preparing for the exam will help you develop all aspects of your playing in a structured way – increasing your knowledge of guitar techniques and music theory.

To download a free information booklet about RGT exams, visit the RGT website: **www.RGT.org.**

CONTENTS

PERFORMANCE TIPS

Sunshine of Your Love – Cream

The original Cream recording started with a riff from the D blues scale, but the RGT arrangement starts with a descending A blues scale riff. The arrangement in this key allows for the use of open strings to make the piece more easily accessible for early stage level players to perform.

The double stops that appear in measure (bar) 3 of the introduction and in the verse can be fingered in a number of ways. Those occurring in measures 3 and 5 can be played either with one finger holding down both strings, or by using two separate fingers. Whichever method is used, make sure that the riffs are played smoothly and fluently.

The double stops in measure 7 are trickier to execute, so try and adopt a fingering approach that allows the note transition to be smooth and with a minimum of string noise.

The chorus features rests (i.e. silences) between the chords in measures 11 and 12. Look out for these when playing the chorus and make sure that your strings are silent between the chord changes.

The two measures of E5 that are played at the end of the chorus feature two different rhythms. Follow the notation and listen to the recorded track carefully to ensure that they are played correctly.

Smoke on the Water – Deep Purple

The RGT arrangement of this piece is in the original key of G minor. The double-stopped opening riff is arranged to be played starting with open strings – rather than fretted like the original Deep Purple recording – in order to make it more suitable for early stage players. Care should be taken to adopt a fingering approach for the rest of the opening riff that allows it to be performed smoothly and fluently, particularly when moving between the pairs of notes on frets 3, 5 and 6 in measure 2.

The verse comprises G5 and F5 power chords with eighth-note rests appearing in a number of places. Practice this section carefully and make sure the power chords are not allowed to ring out across these rests.

The jump between the two power chords in the chorus involves simultaneously changing strings and fret position, so it may need extra practice. Try to ensure that the C5 power chord rings out for the full 4 beats before changing to the A♭5 power chord.

Smells Like Teen Spirit – Nirvana

Instead of the key of F minor used in the original Nirvana recording, the RGT arrangement of this piece is in E minor. This makes it more suitable for early stage players to perform, as the opening riff can then be played starting with open position power chords.

The main riff featured in the introduction and the chorus has been slightly simplified from the original recording by omitting the "ghost" notes and muted strings. You can include these into your performance if you wish, but the core rhythm and fluency of the riff are the most important elements to capture at this level.

The open-string notes that comprise the pre-verse and verse should be allowed to ring into each other as the notation indicates. Notice how the open-string riffs in these sections all start on beat 2, rather than on the first beat.

The middle section features a jump from the low F note on the sixth string to the third string for a half-step string bend. Some extra practice might be needed here to execute the string bend smoothly.

Day Tripper – The Beatles

The RGT arrangement of this piece is in the original key of E major. The opening riff moves smoothly across the three bass strings and is repeated five times before the verse starts. Count the repeats carefully and listen for the lead guitar playing the vocal melody as the cue for the beginning of the verse.

The move from the last note of the verse in measure 10 to the first F#5 power chord in the chorus is tricky to execute smoothly so practice this transition carefully. There are two different rhythm patterns used on the chords in the chorus. Follow the notation carefully and listen to the recorded track to ensure you are familiar with how they are to be played.

The riff that occurs in the bridge (i.e. measures 23 and 24) may require practice to perform smoothly – as a shift of fingerboard position may be required to reach all the notes – so you'll need to take care to adopt a fingering approach that enables fluency and accuracy.

Wonderful Tonight – Eric Clapton

The RGT arrangement of this piece is in the original key of G major. There are several different guitar parts on the original artist's version of this track. The RGT arrangement combines elements of several of these parts. Follow the notation carefully throughout to ensure that your performance is accurate to the RGT arrangement.

The slow tempo and ballad feel of this tune means the pitch accuracy of the string bends in the opening riff is particularly important. Similarly, the slide and hammer-on in measure 8 both need to be executed smoothly and cleanly as demonstrated on the recording.

In the opening measure of the verse (measure 9) the high D at fret 10 should be held down and allowed to ring out for a count of three beats. While this note is ringing, the open string pattern on the D, G and B strings can be picked. (Note that, if preferred, this open string pattern in measure 9 can be omitted from the performance to ensure a smooth transition to the D chord in measure 10.)

Care is needed for the chord changes that occur throughout the remainder of the verse, chorus and bridge sections to ensure they are executed smoothly and cleanly. Practice the chords carefully to maintain an even picking pattern.

Should I Stay or Should I Go – The Clash

The RGT arrangement of this piece is in the original key of D major. The damped D chord in measure 2 is performed by resting the fingers of the fretting hand gently against the strings while strumming. Count the rhythm carefully in measure 4 to ensure the hammer-on is played correctly on the third beat of this measure.

The open string "vamps" that occur between a number of the chord changes throughout the piece help to maintain the energy and fluency of the music. However, the chord changes still need to be executed smoothly and fluently, especially the tricky move from the G chord to the F chord that occurs in measure 11.

Follow the notation and listen to the recorded track carefully in the chorus to ensure you are familiar with the rhythm patterns that are required here. The chords need to change smoothly here and the rhythm is quite tricky to execute at first. In particular the move from the G chord to the F chord and back to the G chord in measures 21 and 22 will require some careful practice to execute smoothly.

The track features a number of rests between chords. Look out for these when playing and make sure you silence the strings when a rest is notated.

All Right Now – Free

The RGT arrangement of this piece is in the original key of A major. The four-bar riff that is featured in the intro and verse sections starts with an open position A major chord. In order to transition smoothly and fluently into the D/A chord that follows, it is recommended that you play the A major chord using the first finger of your fretting hand. This keeps your second and third fingers free to fret the remaining notes needed for the D/A chord.

In the third measure, in addition to the subtle chord change that occurs, there is the added challenge of reproducing the rhythm accurately. Care needs to be taken to ensure that only the B, G and D strings are sounded when strumming this pattern. The rhythm itself is also quite tricky, so listen to the recorded track carefully to ensure that you are familiar with how this section should sound.

The chorus uses mainly power chords played on the D and G strings. In some places, rests (i.e. silences) often occur between chords, so where rests are marked in the notation make sure you either bring your picking hand against the strings to stop them from ringing out or release the pressure with the fretting hand to create the same result.

The instrumental section in this arrangement is an abridged and slightly simplified version of the guitar solo featured in the original version of the song. Consider carefully which finger to use for the slide up from fret 3 to fret 10 in measures 27 and 28, as you will need to be ready for the faster phrase that follows it. These faster, hammer-on phrases in measures 29 and 31 will need practice to ensure the rhythm is smooth and even – listen to the recorded track for confirmation of how the rhythm should sound here.

Paranoid – Black Sabbath

The RGT arrangement of this piece is in the original key of E minor. The eight-measure introduction to this track features a series of hammer-ons. The notation and recorded track will need to be followed carefully here to ensure that the rhythm is performed accurately. The first three hammer-ons are played as quickly as possible whereas the hammer-ons in measure 2 have an even, half-beat rhythm. There is also an added challenge in the first measure where the rhythm is syncopated. Listen to the recorded track carefully to ensure you are familiar with how this should sound.

Power chords then dominate the track with a fast, even rhythm to provide energy and momentum to the music. The abbreviation 'PM' in the notation indicates the use of "palm muting" – place the side edge of your picking hand gently against the bass strings at the bridge. You should still be able to strum the bass strings although the strumming movement will be restricted a little. When played with a distorted guitar sound, this will give you the classic "chugging" rhythm of this track. Follow the notation and practice carefully to ensure that you start and stop this palm-muting technique in the correct places.

Although the bridge section only contains two different power chords, each one ringing out for two measures, be sure to count the beats in this section carefully. Each chord should ring out for eight beats in total. Count these off and then confidently strike the next chord.

Pinball Wizard – The Who

The RGT arrangement of this piece moves through the same keys as the original artist's recording, beginning in B minor.

The three-note chords featured in the introduction should be allowed to ring out for the whole measure. The rhythm gets more complex in the final three measures, so listen to the recorded track and follow the notation carefully.

The rhythm part that is notated for the second introduction and the verse is performed on an acoustic guitar on the original artist's recording. Our recorded track features an electric guitar throughout. Keep your strumming as light and smooth as possible here to ensure an even flow of the rhythm – don't grip the pick too tightly as this may cause the rhythm to falter. The first and seventh chords in each measure feature an accent mark (>) above the notation. On these accented chords try to slightly emphasize the chord by strumming it a little harder – don't overdo it as you might lose the flow of the rhythm. The biggest challenge in this section is maintaining the stamina required to keep up the rhythm across all of the chord changes. Take it slowly at first and focus on one chord at a time before trying to play the entire verse all the way through.

The riff that comes in at measure 20 is an instrumental break in the track so try to strum the chords here with some energy – though not at the expense of the notated rhythm. Take care to follow the rests that occur here and make sure the strings are silent when rests are indicated in the notation.

The penultimate measure of the chorus contains a variation of the D chord that produces a Dsus4 chord by moving the note on fret 7 of the B string up to fret 8. In order to ensure this chord transition sounds as smooth as possible, try to keep the rest of the D chord in place as you move your little finger up one fret.

Sunshine of Your Love

Words and Music by Jack Bruce, Pete Brown and Eric Clapton

Smoke on the Water

Words and Music by Ritchie Blackmore, Ian Gillan, Roger Glover, Jon Lord and Ian Paice

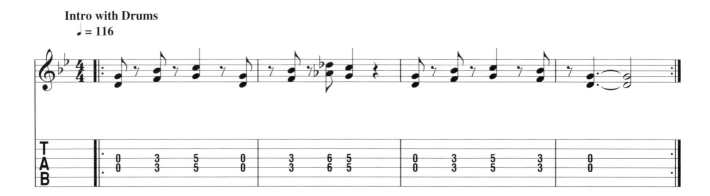

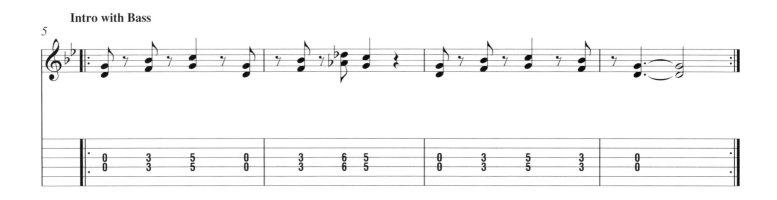

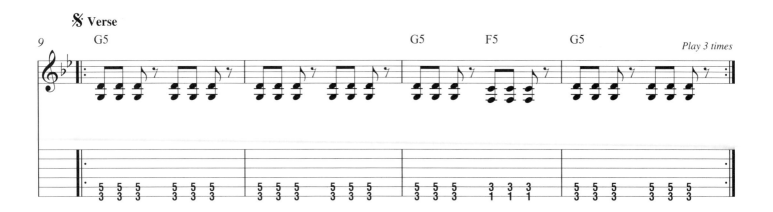

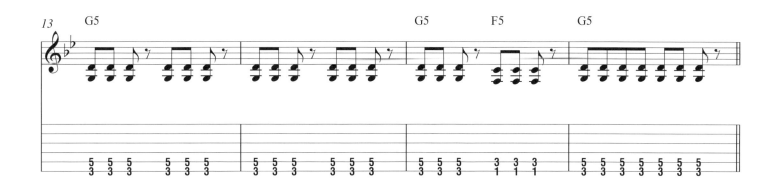

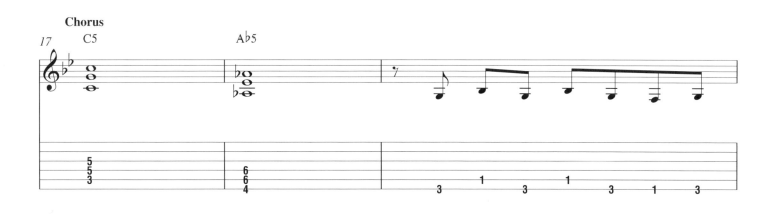

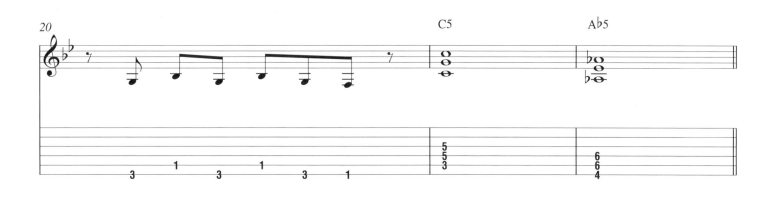

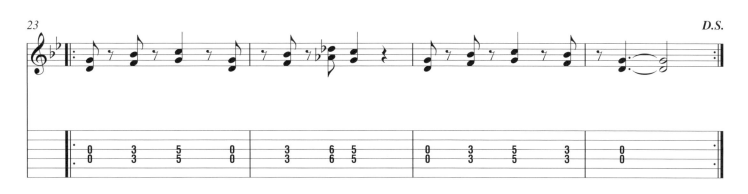

Smells Like Teen Spirit

Words and Music by Kurt Cobain, Krist Novoselic and Dave Grohl

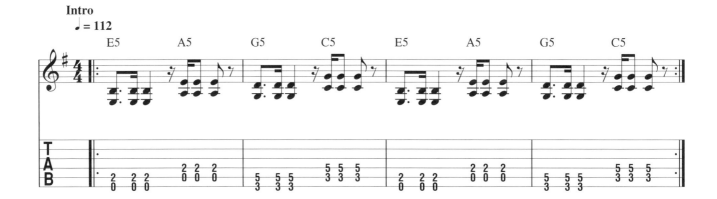

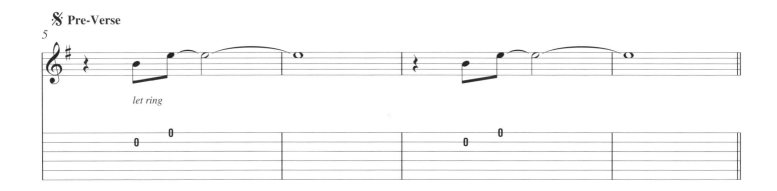

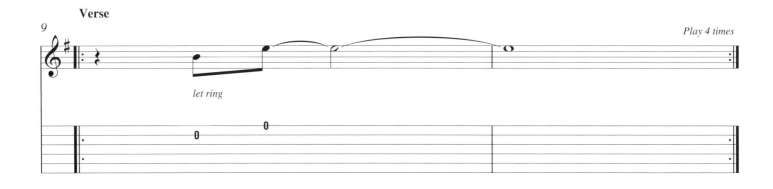

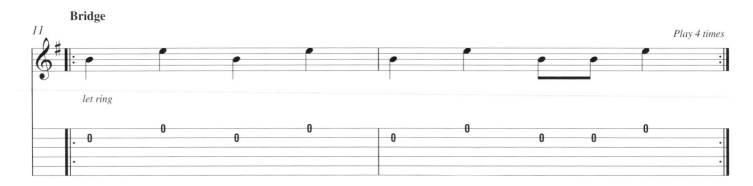

Chorus

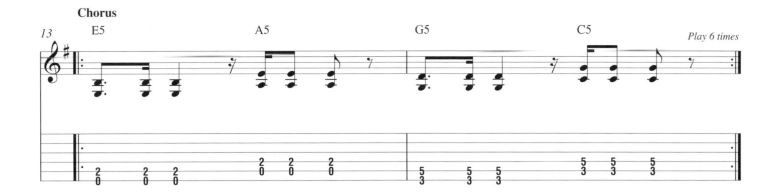

Middle Section

D.S. al Fine
(take repeats)

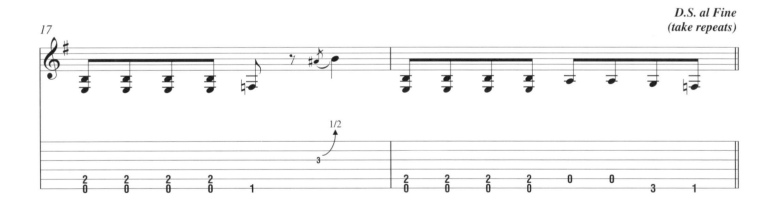

Fine

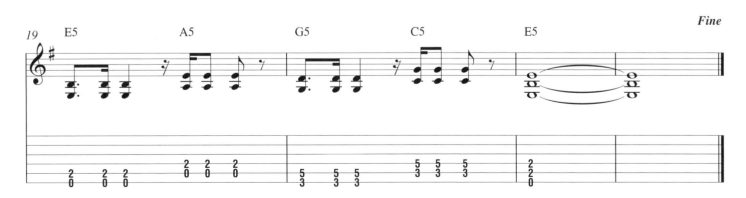

Day Tripper

Words and Music by John Lennon and Paul McCartney

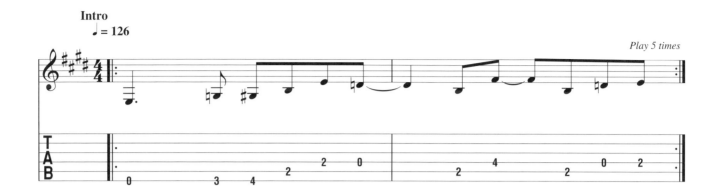

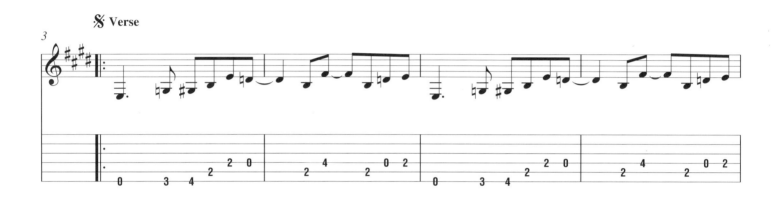

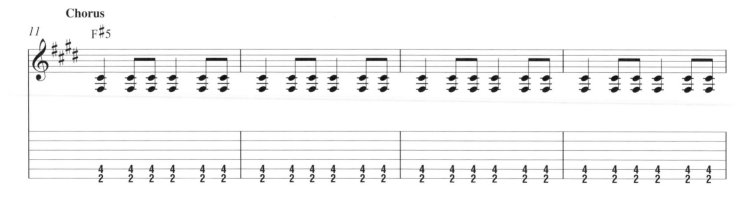

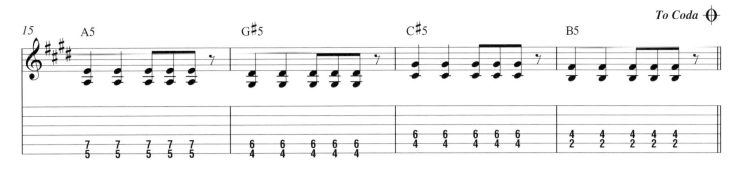

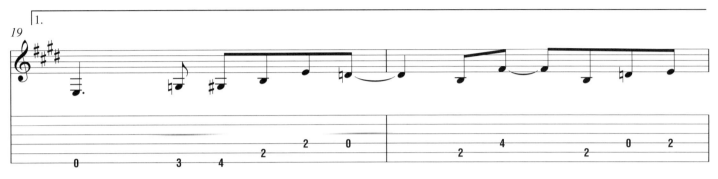

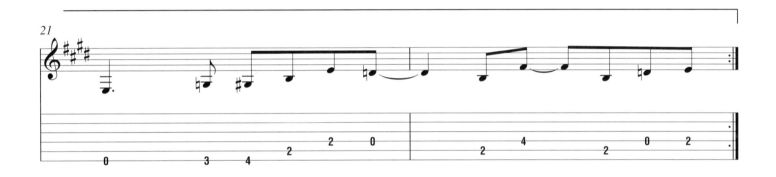

Wonderful Tonight

Words and Music by Eric Clapton

Should I Stay or Should I Go

Words and Music by Mick Jones and Joe Strummer

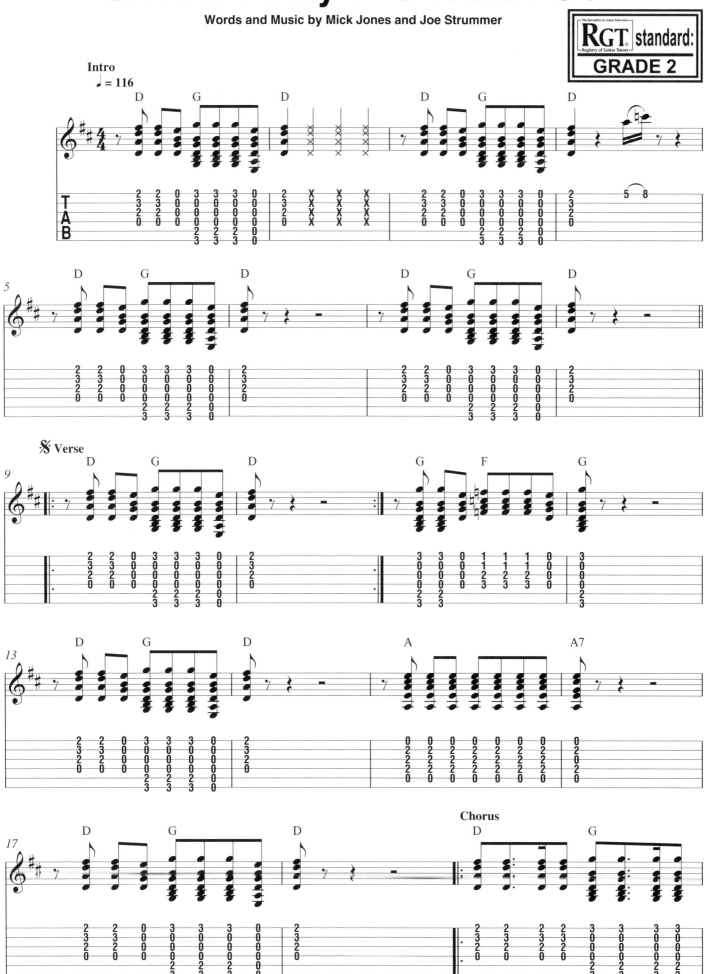

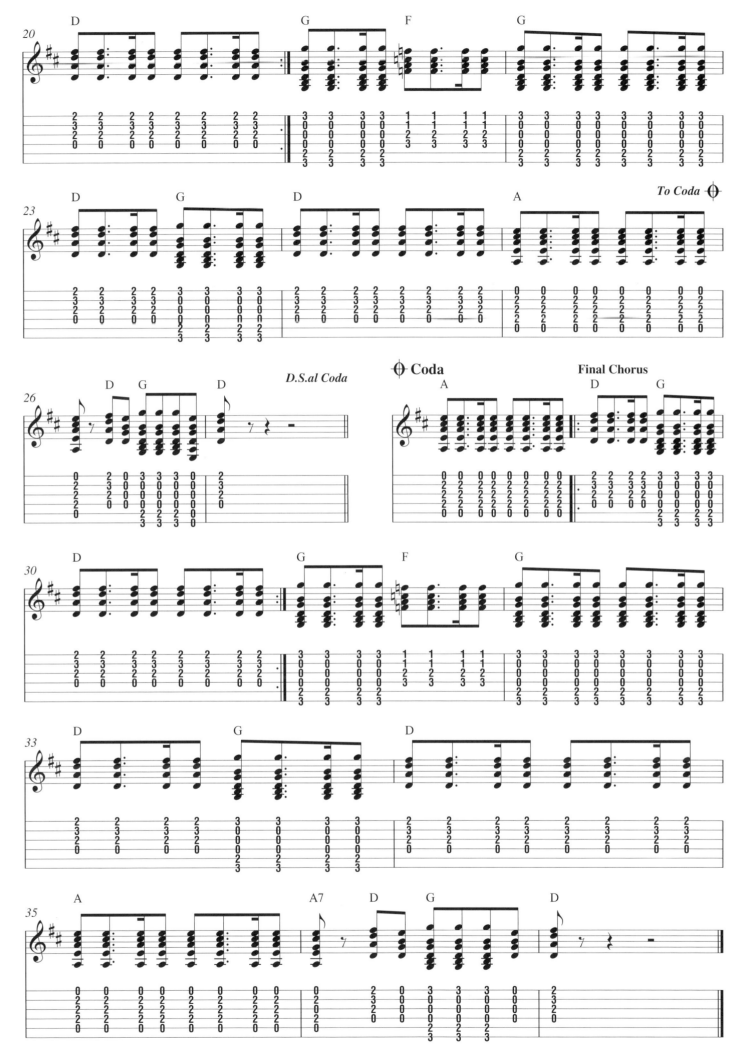

All Right Now

Words and Music by Andy Fraser and Paul Rodgers

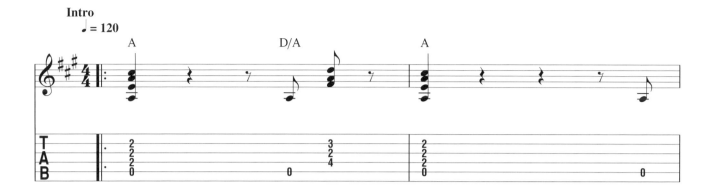

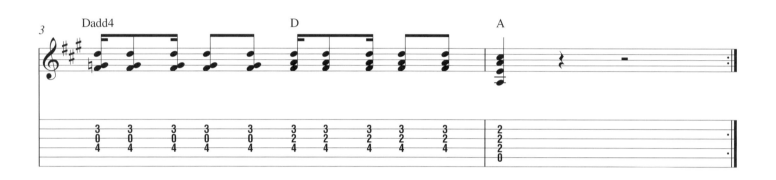

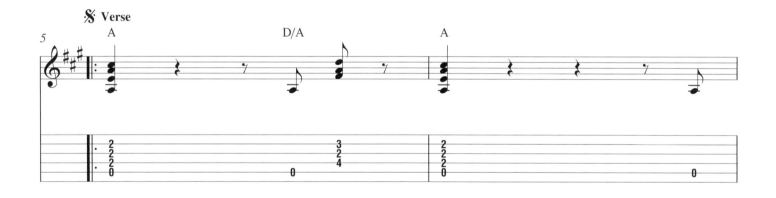

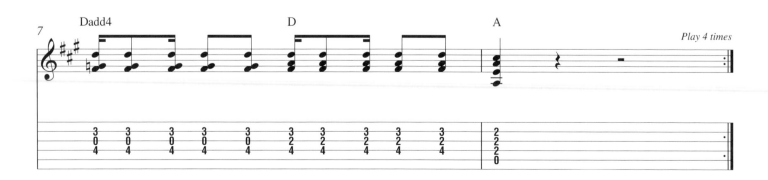

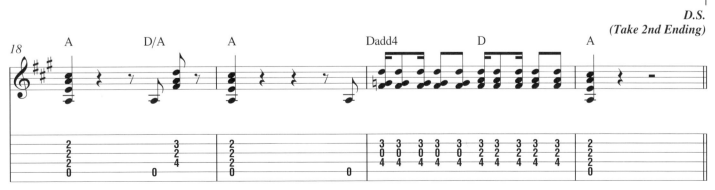

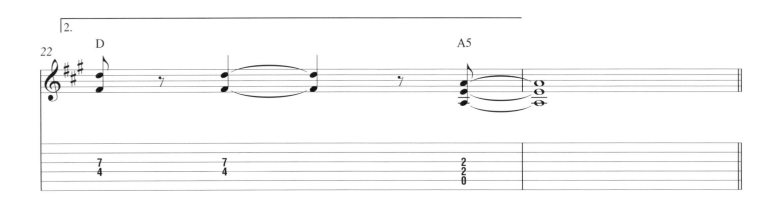

Instrumental section

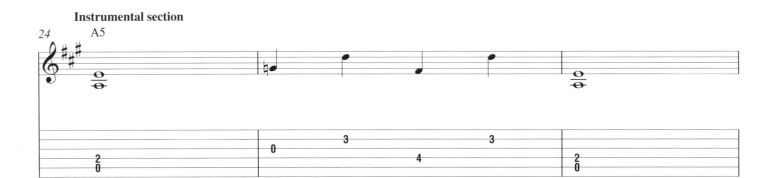

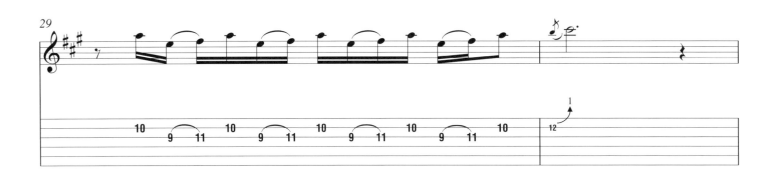

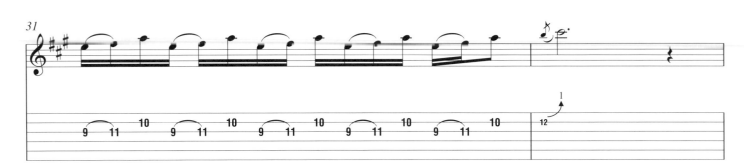

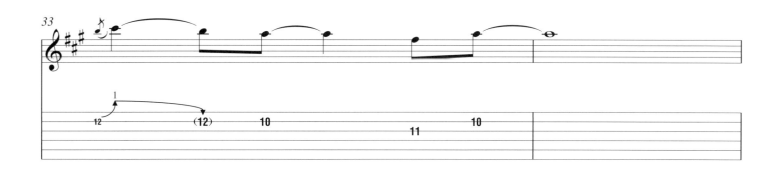

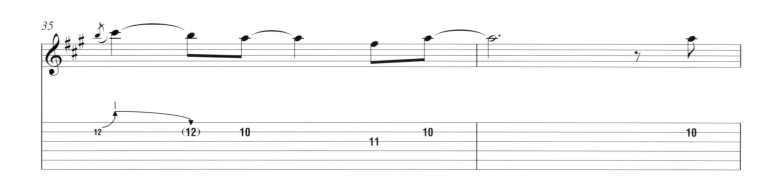

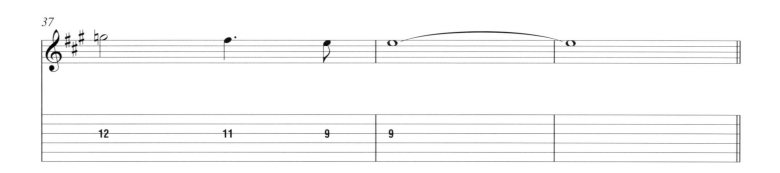

Chorus

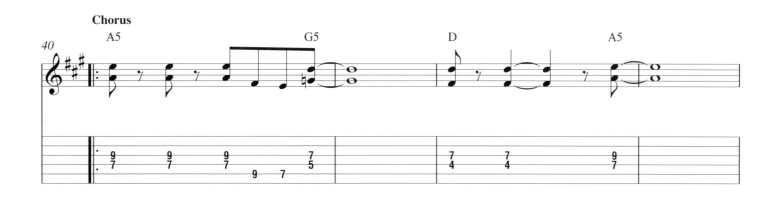

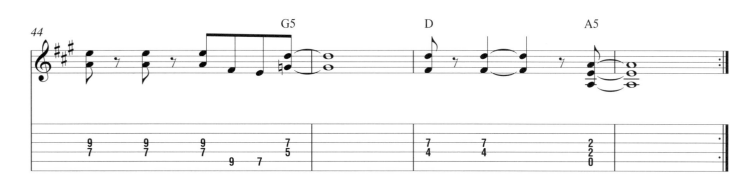

Paranoid

Words and Music by Anthony Iommi, John Osbourne, William Ward and Terence Butler

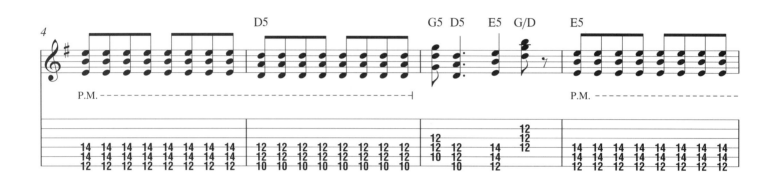

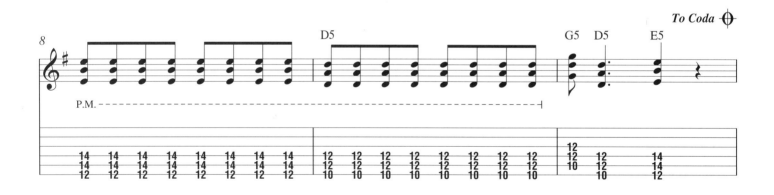

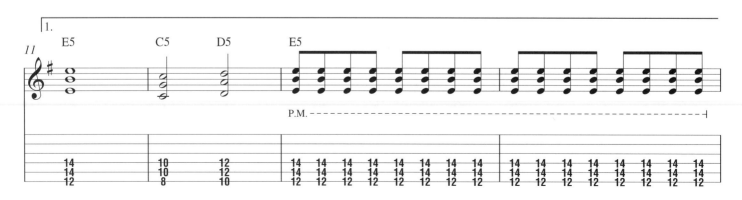

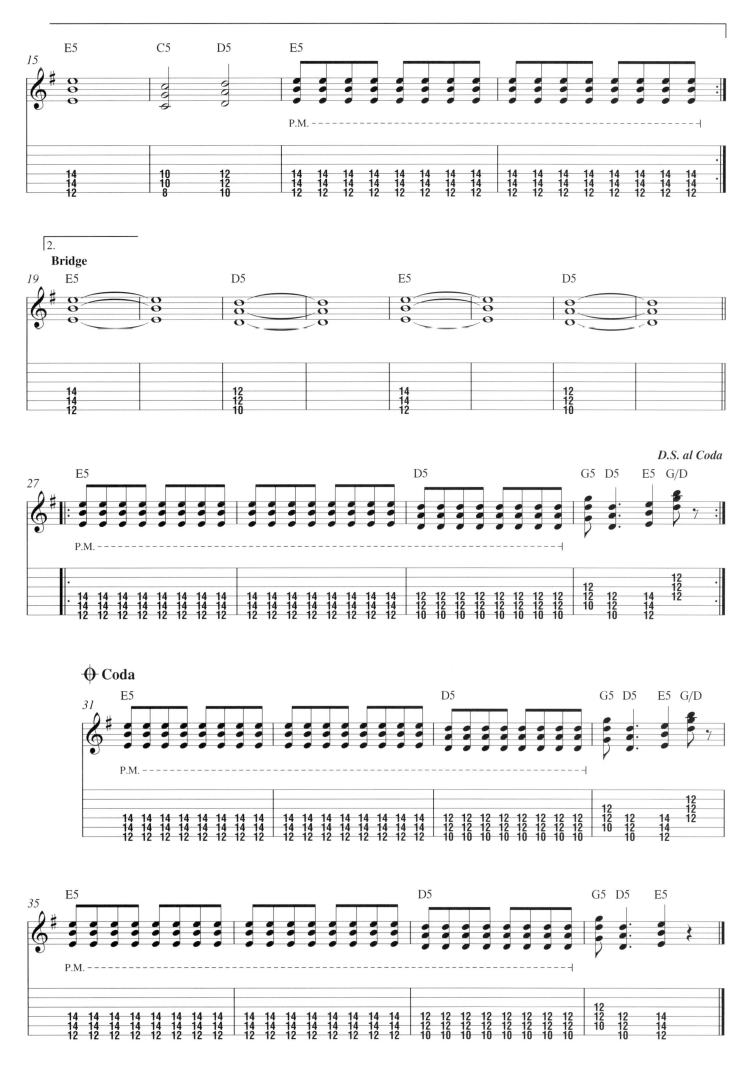

Pinball Wizard

Words and Music by Peter Townshend

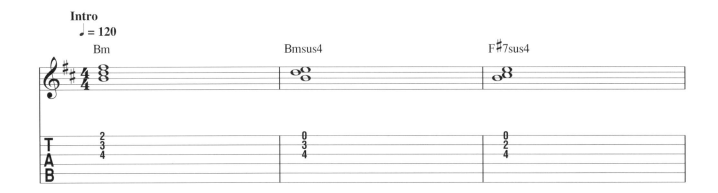

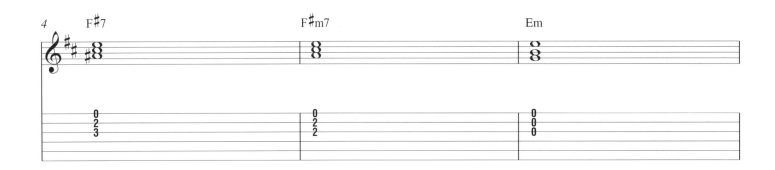

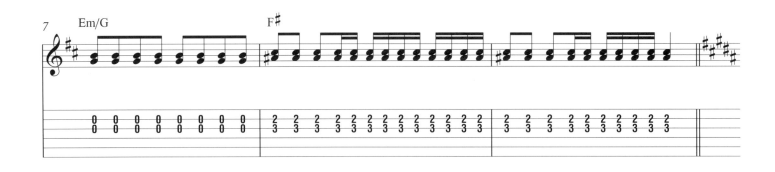

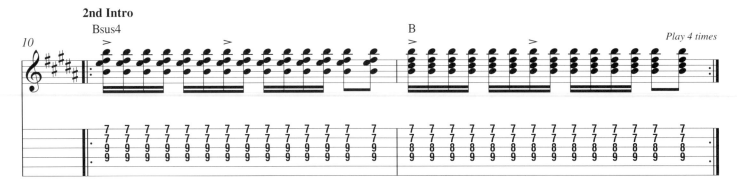

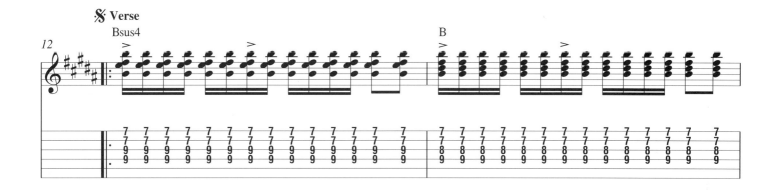

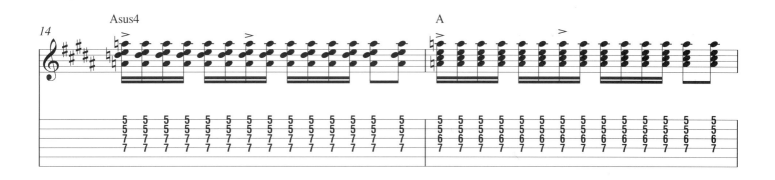

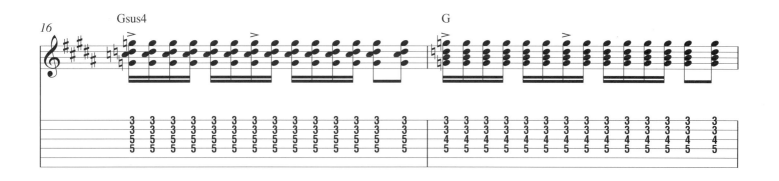

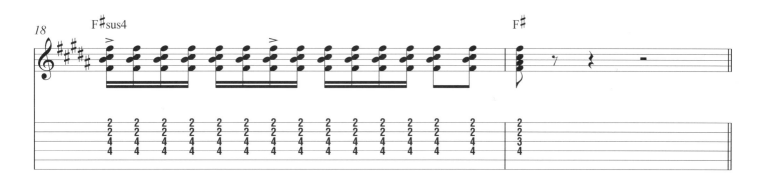

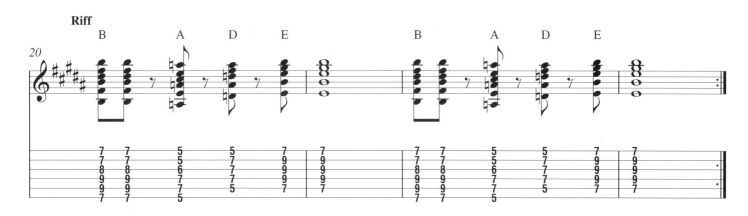

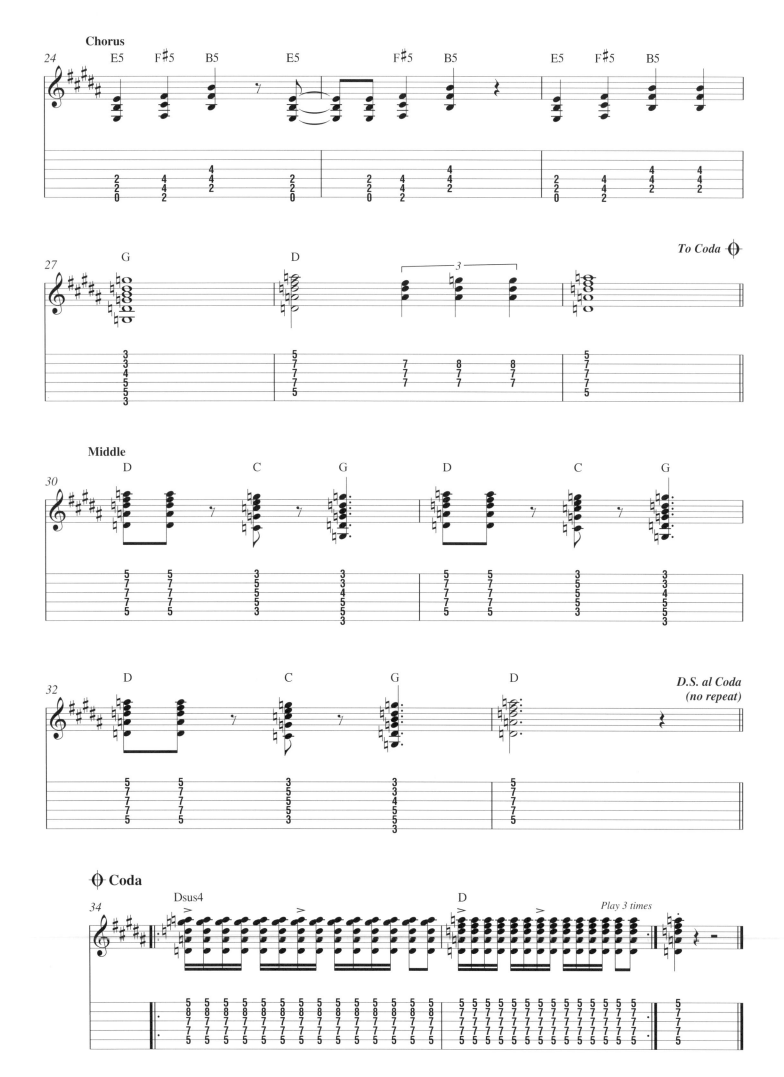

Get Better at Guitar

...with these Great Guitar Instruction Books from Hal Leonard!

101 GUITAR TIPS
 INCLUDES TAB

STUFF ALL THE PROS KNOW AND USE
by Adam St. James

This book contains invaluable guidance on everything from scales and music theory to truss rod adjustments, proper recording studio set-ups, and much more. The book also features snippets of advice from some of the most celebrated guitarists and producers in the music business, including B.B. King, Steve Vai, Joe Satriani, Warren Haynes, Laurence Juber, Pete Anderson, Tom Dowd and others, culled from the author's hundreds of interviews.
00695737 Book/CD Pack.........................$16.95

AMAZING PHRASING
INCLUDES TAB

50 WAYS TO IMPROVE YOUR IMPROVISATIONAL SKILLS
by Tom Kolb

This book/CD pack explores all the main components necessary for crafting well-balanced rhythmic and melodic phrases. It also explains how these phrases are put together to form cohesive solos. Many styles are covered – rock, blues, jazz, fusion, country, Latin, funk and more – and all of the concepts are backed up with musical examples. The companion CD contains 89 demos for listening, and most tracks feature full-band backing.
00695583 Book/CD Pack.........................$19.95

BLUES YOU CAN USE
INCLUDES TAB

by John Ganapes

A comprehensive source designed to help guitarists develop both lead and rhythm playing. Covers: Texas, Delta, R&B, early rock and roll, gospel, blues/rock and more. Includes: 21 complete solos • chord progressions and riffs • turnarounds • moveable scales and more. CD features leads and full band backing.
00695007 Book/CD Pack.........................$19.95

FRETBOARD MASTERY
INCLUDES TAB

by Troy Stetina

Untangle the mysterious regions of the guitar fretboard and unlock your potential. *Fretboard Mastery* familiarizes you with all the shapes you need to know by applying them in real musical examples, thereby reinforcing and reaffirming your newfound knowledge. The result is a much higher level of comprehension and retention.
00695331 Book/CD Pack.........................$19.95

FRETBOARD ROADMAPS – 2ND EDITION

ESSENTIAL GUITAR PATTERNS THAT ALL THE PROS KNOW AND USE
by Fred Sokolow

The updated edition of this bestseller features more songs, updated lessons, and a full audio CD! Learn to play lead and rhythm anywhere on the fretboard, in any key; play a variety of lead guitar styles; play chords and progressions anywhere on the fretboard; expand your chord vocabulary; and learn to think musically – the way the pros do.
00695941 Book/CD Pack.........................$14.95

GUITAR AEROBICS
 INCLUDES TAB

A 52-WEEK, ONE-LICK-PER-DAY WORKOUT PROGRAM FOR DEVELOPING, IMPROVING & MAINTAINING GUITAR TECHNIQUE
by Troy Nelson

From the former editor of *Guitar One* magazine, here is a daily dose of vitamins to keep your chops fine tuned! Musical styles include rock, blues, jazz, metal, country, and funk. Techniques taught include alternate picking, arpeggios, sweep picking, string skipping, legato, string bending, and rhythm guitar. These exercises will increase speed, and improve dexterity and pick- and fret-hand accuracy. The accompanying CD includes all 365 workout licks plus play-along grooves in every style at eight different metronome settings.
00695946 Book/CD Pack.........................$19.95

GUITAR CLUES
 INCLUDES TAB

OPERATION PENTATONIC
by Greg Koch

Join renowned guitar master Greg Koch as he clues you in to a wide variety of fun and valuable pentatonic scale applications. Whether you're new to improvising or have been doing it for a while, this book/CD pack will provide loads of delicious licks and tricks that you can use right away, from volume swells and chicken pickin' to intervallic and chordal ideas. The CD includes 65 demo and play-along tracks.
00695827 Book/CD Pack.........................$19.95

INTRODUCTION TO GUITAR TONE & EFFECTS

by David M. Brewster

This book/CD pack teaches the basics of guitar tones and effects, with audio examples on CD. Readers will learn about: overdrive, distortion and fuzz • using equalizers • modulation effects • reverb and delay • multi-effect processors • and more.
00695766 Book/CD Pack.........................$14.95

PICTURE CHORD ENCYCLOPEDIA

This comprehensive guitar chord resource for all playing styles and levels features five voicings of 44 chord qualities for all twelve keys – 2,640 chords in all! For each, there is a clearly illustrated chord frame, as well as *an actual photo* of the chord being played! Includes info on basic fingering principles, open chords and barre chords, partial chords and broken-set forms, and more.
00695224 ....$19.95

SCALE CHORD RELATIONSHIPS
  INCLUDES TAB

by Michael Mueller & Jeff Schroedl

This book teaches players how to determine which scales to play with which chords, so guitarists will never have to fear chord changes again! This book/CD pack explains how to: recognize keys • analyze chord progressions • use the modes • play over nondiatonic harmony • use harmonic and melodic minor scales • use symmetrical scales such as chromatic, whole-tone and diminished scales • incorporate exotic scales such as Hungarian major and Gypsy minor • and much more!
00695563 Book/CD Pack.........................$14.95

SPEED MECHANICS FOR LEAD GUITAR
INCLUDES TAB

Take your playing to the stratosphere with the most advanced lead book by this proven heavy metal author. *Speed Mechanics* is the ultimate technique book for developing the kind of speed and precision in today's explosive playing styles. Learn the fastest ways to achieve speed and control, secrets to make your practice time really count, and how to open your ears and make your musical ideas more solid and tangible. Packed with over 200 vicious exercises including Troy's scorching version of "Flight of the Bumblebee." Music and examples demonstrated on CD. 89-minute audio.
00699323 Book/CD Pack.........................$19.95

TOTAL ROCK GUITAR
  INCLUDES TAB

A COMPLETE GUIDE TO LEARNING ROCK GUITAR
by Troy Stetina

This unique and comprehensive source for learning rock guitar is designed to develop both lead and rhythm playing. It covers: getting a tone that rocks • open chords, power chords and barre chords • riffs, scales and licks • string bending, strumming, palm muting, harmonics and alternate picking • all rock styles • and much more. The examples are in standard notation with chord grids and tab, and the CD includes full-band backing for all 22 songs.
00695246 Book/CD Pack.........................$19.99

GUITAR PLAY-ALONG

This series will help you play your favorite songs quickly and easily. Just follow the tab and listen to the CD to hear how the guitar should sound, and then play along using the separate backing tracks. Mac or PC users can also slow down the tempo without changing pitch by using the CD in their computer. The melody and lyrics are included in the book so that you can sing or simply follow along.

INCLUDES TAB

61. SLIPKNOT 00699775.................$14.95	**78. NIRVANA** 00700132.................$16.99	**100. B.B. KING** 00700466 ....$14.99	**119. AC/DC CLASSICS** 00701356 ....$17.99
62. CHRISTMAS CAROLS 00699798.................$12.95	**88. ACOUSTIC ANTHOLOGY** 00700175.................$19.95	**102. CLASSIC PUNK** 00700769.................$14.99	**120. PROGRESSIVE ROCK** 00701457.................$14.99
63. CREEDENCE CLEARWATER REVIVAL 00699802.................$16.99	**81. ROCK ANTHOLOGY** 00700176.................$22.99	**103. SWITCHFOOT** 00700773 ....$16.99	**122. CROSBY, STILLS & NASH** 00701610.................$16.99
64. OZZY OSBOURNE 00699803.................$16.99	**82. EASY ROCK SONGS** 00700177.................$12.99	**104. DUANE ALLMAN** 00700846.................$16.99	**123. LENNON & McCARTNEY ACOUSTIC** 00701614.................$16.99
65. THE DOORS 00699806.................$16.99	**83. THREE CHORD SONGS** 00700178.................$16.99	**106. WEEZER** 00700958 ....$14.99	**124. MODERN WORSHIP** 00701629.................$14.99
66. THE ROLLING STONES 00699807.................$16.95	**84. STEELY DAN** 00700200 ....$16.99	**107. CREAM** 00701069.................$16.99	**126. BOB MARLEY** 00701701.................$16.99
67. BLACK SABBATH 00699808.................$16.99	**85. THE POLICE** 00700269.................$16.99	**108. THE WHO** 00701053 ....$16.99	**127. 1970s ROCK** 00701739.................$14.99
68. PINK FLOYD – DARK SIDE OF THE MOON 00699809.................$16.99	**86. BOSTON** 00700465.................$16.99	**109. STEVE MILLER** 00701054 ....$14.99	**128. 1960s ROCK** 00701740.................$14.99
69. ACOUSTIC FAVORITES 00699810.................$14.95	**87. ACOUSTIC WOMEN** 00700763 ....$14.99	**111. JOHN MELLENCAMP** 00701056 ....$14.99	**129. MEGADETH** 00701741.................$14.99
70. OZZY OSBOURNE 00699805 ....$16.99	**88. GRUNGE** 00700467.................$16.99	**113. JIM CROCE** 00701058 ....$14.99	**130. IRON MAIDEN** 00701742.................$14.99
71. CHRISTIAN ROCK 00699824.................$14.95	**91. BLUES INSTRUMENTALS** 00700505.................$14.99	**114. BON JOVI** 00701060 ....$14.99	**131. 1990s ROCK** 00701743.................$14.99
72. ACOUSTIC '90s 00699827.................$14.95	**92. EARLY ROCK INSTRUMENTALS** 00700506.................$12.99	**115. JOHNNY CASH** 00701070 ....$16.99	**133. TAYLOR SWIFT** 00701894.................$16.99
73. BLUESY ROCK 00699829 ....$16.99	**93. ROCK INSTRUMENTALS** 00700507.................$16.99	**116. THE VENTURES** 00701124 ....$14.99	
74. PAUL BALOCHE 00699831.................$14.95	**96. THIRD DAY** 00700560.................$14.95		
75. TOM PETTY 00699882.................$16.99	**97. ROCK BAND** 00700703.................$14.99		
76. COUNTRY HITS 00699884.................$14.95	**98. ROCK BAND** 00700704.................$14.95		
77. BLUEGRASS 00699910.................$12.99	**99. ZZ TOP** 00700762 ....$16.99		

FOR MORE INFORMATION, SEE YOUR LOCAL MUSIC DEALER,
OR WRITE TO:

7777 W. BLUEMOUND RD. P.O. BOX 13819 MILWAUKEE, WI 53213

For complete songlists, visit Hal Leonard online at
www.halleonard.com

Prices, contents, and availability subject to change without notice.

0311

EASY GUITAR
WITH NOTES & TAB

This series features simplified arrangements with notes, tab, chord charts, and strum and pick patterns.

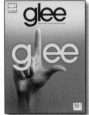

Prices, contents and availability subject to change without notice.

FOR MORE INFORMATION,
SEE YOUR LOCAL MUSIC DEALER,
OR WRITE TO:

HAL•LEONARD®
CORPORATION
7777 W. BLUEMOUND RD. P.O. BOX 13819
MILWAUKEE, WISCONSIN 53213

Visit Hal Leonard online at
www.halleonard.com

MIXED FOLIOS

00702287	Acoustic	$14.99
00702002	Acoustic Rock Hits for Easy Guitar	$12.95
00702166	All-Time Best Guitar Collection	$19.99
00699665	Beatles Best	$12.95
00702232	Best Acoustic Songs for Easy Guitar	$12.99
00702233	Best Hard Rock Songs	$14.99
00698978	Big Christmas Collection	$16.95
00702115	Blues Classics	$10.95
00385020	Broadway Songs for Kids	$9.95
00702237	Christian Acoustic Favorites	$12.95
00702149	Children's Christian Songbook	$7.95
00702028	Christmas Classics	$7.95
00702185	Christmas Hits	$9.95
00702016	Classic Blues for Easy Guitar	$12.95
00702141	Classic Rock	$8.95
00702203	CMT's 100 Greatest Country Songs	$27.95
00702170	Contemporary Christian Christmas	$9.95
00702006	Contemporary Christian Favorites	$9.95
00702065	Contemporary Women of Country	$9.95
00702239	Country Classics for Easy Guitar	$19.99
00702282	Country Hits of 2009-2010	$14.99
00702240	Country Hits of 2007-2008	$12.95
00702225	Country Hits of '06-'07	$12.95
00702085	Disney Movie Hits	$12.95
00702257	Easy Acoustic Guitar Songs	$14.99
00702280	Easy Guitar Tab White Pages	$29.99
00702212	Essential Christmas	$9.95
00702041	Favorite Hymns for Easy Guitar	$9.95
00702281	4 Chord Rock	$9.99
00702286	Glee	$16.99
00702174	God Bless America® & Other Songs for a Better Nation	$8.95
00699374	Gospel Favorites	$14.95
00702160	The Great American Country Songbook	$14.95
00702050	Great Classical Themes for Easy Guitar	$6.95
00702131	Great Country Hits of the '90s	$8.95
00702116	Greatest Hymns for Guitar	$8.95
00702130	The Groovy Years	$9.95
00702184	Guitar Instrumentals	$9.95
00702231	High School Musical for Easy Guitar	$12.95
00702241	High School Musical 2	$12.95
00702046	Hits of the '70s for Easy Guitar	$8.95
00702032	International Songs for Easy Guitar	$12.95
00702275	Jazz Favorites for Easy Guitar	$14.99
00702051	Jock Rock for Easy Guitar	$9.95
00702162	Jumbo Easy Guitar Songbook	$19.95
00702112	Latin Favorites	$9.95
00702258	Legends of Rock	$14.99
00702138	Mellow Rock Hits	$10.95
00702261	Modern Worship Hits	$14.99
00702147	Motown's Greatest Hits	$9.95
00702189	MTV's 100 Greatest Pop Songs	$24.95
00702272	1950s Rock	$14.99
00702271	1960s Rock	$14.99
00702270	1970s Rock	$14.99
00702269	1980s Rock	$14.99
00702268	1990s Rock	$14.99
00702187	Selections from O Brother Where Art Thou?	$12.95
00702178	100 Songs for Kids	$12.95
00702125	Praise and Worship for Guitar	$9.95
00702155	Rock Hits for Guitar	$9.95
00702242	Rock Band	$19.95
00702256	Rock Band 2	$19.99
00702128	Rockin' Down the Highway	$9.95
00702110	The Sound of Music	$9.99
00702285	Southern Rock Hits	$12.99
00702124	Today's Christian Rock – 2nd Edition	$9.95
00702220	Today's Country Hits	$9.95
00702198	Today's Hits for Guitar	$9.95
00702217	Top Christian Hits	$12.95
00702235	Top Christian Hits of '07-'08	$14.95
00702284	Top Hits of 2010	$14.99
00702246	Top Hits of 2008	$12.95
00702206	Very Best of Rock	$9.95
00702255	VH1's 100 Greatest Hard Rock Songs	$27.99
00702175	VH1's 100 Greatest Songs of Rock and Roll	$24.95
00702253	Wicked	$12.99
00702192	Worship Favorites	$9.95

ARTIST COLLECTIONS

00702267	AC/DC for Easy Guitar	$14.99
00702001	Best of Aerosmith	$16.95
00702040	Best of the Allman Brothers	$14.99
00702169	Best of The Beach Boys	$10.95
00702201	The Essential Black Sabbath	$12.95
00702140	Best of Brooks & Dunn	$10.95
00702095	Best of Mariah Carey	$12.95
00702043	Best of Johnny Cash	$14.99
00702033	Best of Steven Curtis Chapman	$14.95
00702263	Best of Casting Crowns	$12.99
00702090	Eric Clapton's Best	$10.95
00702086	Eric Clapton – from the Album Unplugged	$10.95
00702202	The Essential Eric Clapton	$12.95
00702250	blink-182 – Greatest Hits	$12.99
00702053	Best of Patsy Cline	$10.95
00702229	The Very Best of Creedence Clearwater Revival	$12.95
00702145	Best of Jim Croce	$10.95
00702278	Crosby, Stills & Nash	$12.99
00702219	David Crowder*Band Collection	$12.95
00702122	The Doors for Easy Guitar	$12.99
00702276	Fleetwood Mac – Easy Guitar Collection	$12.99
00702099	Best of Amy Grant	$9.95
00702190	Best of Pat Green	$19.95
00702136	Best of Merle Haggard	$12.99
00702243	Hannah Montana	$14.95
00702244	Hannah Montana 2/Meet Miley Cyrus	$16.95
00702227	Jimi Hendrix – Smash Hits	$14.99
00702236	Best of Antonio Carlos Jobim	$12.95
00702087	Best of Billy Joel	$10.95
00702245	Elton John – Greatest Hits 1970-2002	$14.99
00702204	Robert Johnson	$9.95
00702277	Best of Jonas Brothers	$14.99
00702234	Selections from Toby Keith – 35 Biggest Hits	$12.95
00702003	Kiss	$9.95
00702193	Best of Jennifer Knapp	$12.95
00702097	John Lennon – Imagine	$9.95
00702216	Lynyrd Skynyrd	$15.99
00702182	The Essential Bob Marley	$12.95
00702248	Paul McCartney – All the Best	$14.99
00702129	Songs of Sarah McLachlan	$12.95
02501316	Metallica – Death Magnetic	$15.95
00702209	Steve Miller Band – Young Hearts (Greatest Hits)	$12.95
00702096	Best of Nirvana	$14.95
00702211	The Offspring – Greatest Hits	$12.95
00702030	Best of Roy Orbison	$12.95
00702144	Best of Ozzy Osbourne	$12.95
00702279	Tom Petty	$12.99
00702139	Elvis Country Favorites	$9.95
00699415	Best of Queen for Guitar	$14.99
00702208	Red Hot Chili Peppers – Greatest Hits	$12.95
00702093	Rolling Stones Collection	$17.95
00702092	Best of the Rolling Stones	$14.99
00702196	Best of Bob Seger	$12.95
00702252	Frank Sinatra – Nothing But the Best	$12.99
00702010	Best of Rod Stewart	$14.95
00702150	Best of Sting	$12.95
00702049	Best of George Strait	$12.95
00702259	Taylor Swift for Easy Guitar	$12.99
00702290	Taylor Swift – Speak Now	$12.99
00702223	Chris Tomlin – Arriving	$12.95
00702262	Chris Tomlin Collection	$14.99
00702226	Chris Tomlin – See the Morning	$12.95
00702132	Shania Twain – Greatest Hits	$10.95
00702108	Best of Stevie Ray Vaughan	$10.95
00702123	Best of Hank Williams	$12.99
00702111	Stevie Wonder – Guitar Collection	$9.95
00702228	Neil Young – Greatest Hits	$12.99
00702188	Essential ZZ Top	$10.95

0211